William Augustus Muhlenberg

Testimony of Jesus - The Spirit of Prophecy

Sermon Preached at the Re-Opening of the Church of Augustus

William Augustus Muhlenberg

Testimony of Jesus - The Spirit of Prophecy
Sermon Preached at the Re-Opening of the Church of Augustus

ISBN/EAN: 9783337103842

Printed in Europe, USA, Canada, Australia, Japan

Cover: Foto ©Lupo / pixelio.de

More available books at **www.hansebooks.com**

A SERMON

PREACHED AT THE RE-OPENING

OF THE

CHURCH OF AUGUSTUS

(EVANGELICAL LUTHERAN),

Trappe, Montgomery Co., Pennsylvania,

SEPTEMBER 5, 1860.

BY WILLIAM AUGUSTUS MUHLENBERG,

SENIOR PASTOR OF THE CHURCH OF THE HOLY COMMUNION, AND PASTOR AND SUPERINTENDENT
OF ST. LUKE'S HOSPITAL, NEW YORK.

PUBLISHED BY REQUEST.

NEW YORK:
ROBERT CRAIGHEAD, PRINTER.
1861.

RESTORATION

OF THE

OLD EVANGELICAL LUTHERAN "CHURCH OF AUGUSTUS,"

AT TRAPPE, MONTGOMERY COUNTY, PA.

In the year 1851, the Evangelical Lutheran Congregation in Providence township, Montgomery Co., Pa., then worshipping in the old "Church of Augustus," which was erected in 1743, under the pastoral care of Henry Melchior Muhlenberg, D.D., resolved to erect a new and more commodious church edifice, for the better accommodation of the large and constantly increasing congregation.

Accordingly, on the 8th day of August, 1852, the corner-stone of the new building was laid with appropriate ceremonies, and on the 6th day of November, 1853, it was solemnly consecrated to the service of Almighty God. Rev. J. W. Richards, D.D., a grandson of the venerable Dr. Muhlenberg, officiated at the laying of the corner-stone, and Rev. John C. Baker, D.D., assisted by Rev. Dr. Richards and Rev. G. A. Wenzel (Pastor Loci), performed the ceremonies at the Consecration.

After the dedication and opening of the new Sanctuary, the old one was no longer used as a place of worship, except for Sunday School purposes, the commodious new edifice being much better adapted to the wants of the congregation.

Dr. H. H. Muhlenberg, of Reading, Pa., also a descendant of the founder of the church, at the time the old church was about being vacated by the congregation, generously contributed one hundred dollars towards keeping it in repair.

In the spring of 1859, prior to the annual opening of the Sunday School, the roof and ceiling of the old church were examined, and found to be in such condition as to render the occupancy of the building unsafe. The Sunday School was then transferred to the new church.

On the 16th of February, 1860, a violent storm carried away a portion of the roof, and left the walls standing in a very exposed and unsightly condition. Too many hallowed associations clustered around the venerable pile, to allow its complete destruction, and accordingly on the 28th of February, a congregational meeting was held to consult in reference to its condition. There being a diversity of opinion as to the propriety of repairing it, and thereby increasing the debt already incurred in the building of the new edifice, no definite action was had in the matter, excepting the appointment of Committees to estimate the cost of re-construction, and to ascertain the probable amount of money that could be raised for that object. The meeting reassembled on the 13th of March, when, after hearing the reports of the Committees, it was resolved " That the whole matter of repairing the old church be placed in the hands of an Executive Committee of the friends of the measure, who should have full power to make such repairs as they deemed proper, being careful to retain as nearly as possible the original external appearance of the building, *Provided*, the funds be collected without drawing upon the Treasury of the Congregation." Messrs. S. GROSS FRY, HORACE ROYER, and REV. G. SILL, Pastor, were designated as the Committee.

The success of the Committee in obtaining contributions towards the project was at first in nowise flattering. After addressing a number of those who the Committee supposed would feel a common interest in preserving the Ancient Temple of their Fathers from the destruction that was impending, and receiving so little encouragement, it was feared that they would not be warranted in proceeding with the work.

Finally, an appeal was made to the Rev. Wm. Augustus Muhlenberg, D.D., a great-grandson of the illustrious patriarch, at present the Pastor of the Church of the Holy Communion (P.E.) in New York City, and founder of St. Luke's Hospital, who generously replied that " he, through his sister, Mrs. Rogers, and other members of the family, would gladly extend to the Committee the aid desired in securing the venerable old building from its impending ruin." The work was at once commenced, and the necessary repairs speedily accomplished ; and the venerable structure, having renewed her strength, again stands ready for any service which the congregation may appoint for her, and which will be consistent with her hallowed history.

The Committee deeming it proper that some formal exercises should be held at the re-opening of the old church, the fifth and sixth days of September were set apart for that purpose, and the Rev. Dr. Muhlenberg, who had so cheerfully responded to the request of the Committee, was invited to be present and deliver the Re-opening address. The invitation was accepted, and on Wednesday morning, the fifth of September, the excellent and appropriate discourse herein contained was delivered by Dr. Muhlenberg to an immense congregation from the same pulpit filled by his great-grandfather, more than one hundred years ago.

The German discourse of the occasion was preached from the same pulpit on the morning following, by Rev. Dr. W. Julius Mann, of Philadelphia, President of the Pennsylvania Synod. Interesting exercises were held also in the evening, Rev. Jacob Fry, Pastor of the First Lutheran Church, Carlisle, Pa. (who is from this congregation, and was confirmed in the old church), delivered an address preparatory to the re-opening exercises on the evening of the 4th; and on the following evening, Rev. E. W. Hutter, Pastor of St. Matthew's Lutheran Church of Philadelphia, officiated. Besides 'the clergymen already mentioned, there were present on the occasion, Revs. G. F. Miller, C. A. Baer, J. W. Hassler, Wm. Weaver, H. Wendt and J. F. Wampole of the Lutheran Church, and Rev. Dr. Cruse and Rev. Mr Millett, of the Episcopal Church, and Rev. Messrs. Dechant and Kooken of the German Reformed Church.

A brief sketch of the History of the Church was read by the Pastor (Rev. Mr. Sill) on the morning of the fifth, a copy of which is also contained in this publication.

By the Committee.

S. Gross Fry, Chairman.

A BRIEF SKETCH

OF THE HISTORY OF THE OLD "CHURCH OF AUGUSTUS."

READ TO THE CONGREGATION ON THE MORNING OF SEPTEMBER 5, AS PART
OF THE EXERCISES, BY THE PASTOR, REV. G. SILL.

THROUGH the mercy of the kind providence of God, we are permitted this day to assemble within the walls of this ancient and venerable temple, where for more than a century the gospel has been proclaimed, to open it again for religious worship. It may not be uninteresting to many present on this occasion, to give a brief historical account of the church, the names of the ministers, when, and how long they served as pastors of the congregation worshipping in this house.

The corner-stone of the present edifice was laid on the second day of May, A.D. 1743, with the following dedicatory inscription placed in the church wall: "Sub remigio Christi has ædes Societati Augustanæ confess: deditæ dedicatas ex ipso fundamento exstruxit Henricus Melchior Muhlenberg, una cum censoribus, J. N. Crossmanno, F. Marstellero, A. Heilmano, J. Muellero, H. Hasio, et G. Rebnero A.D. M.DCC.XLIII."

The work progressed rapidly, for by the thirty-first of August the building was under roof, and the congregation, heretofore worshipping in a barn, moved into the church, and for the first time held service in it on the twelfth day of September of the same year.

It was determined not to dedicate the church until entirely finished, which was not effected until A.D. 1745; and on either the last Sunday in September, or the first in October, of the same year, it was solemnly dedicated to the worship of the Triune God.

It was regularly occupied for divine service until the autumn of 1853, when the congregation moved into the large and commodious brick church erected by them on these grounds. From that time up to the present it has been occupied by the Sunday School, with the exception of the two last years, when it was not considered safe for occupancy.

The respective ministers who officiated in this church from its commencement, were

First. Dr. Henry Melchior Muhlenberg, the founder of the church. He commenced his labors here in November, 1742, and continued until October, 1761, when he moved with his family to Philadelphia.

Second. The Rev. Mr. Hartwig became his successor, but only remained until April, 1762.

Third. Rev. Jacob Van Buskerk took charge of the congregation in May, 1762, and served for two years, when he dropped this and continued serving the other congregation (New Hanover) connected with this charge for one year, during which time the Trappe congregation was without a settled minister.

Fourth. In December, 1765, the Rev. John Ludwig Voigt became pastor, and continued his service until about the year 1798. During his ministry in this church, Dr. Muhlenberg moved back again to the Trappe (viz. in 1776), where he remained until his useful and eventful life closed, on the 7th day of October, 1787.

Fifth. The Rev. Mr. Weinland succeeded Mr. Voigt, in 1798, and remained pastor of the congregation until 1808, when he was removed from his labors by death.

Sixth. After Mr. Weinland's death, the congregation was served for several months as a supply by the Rev. Frederick William Geisenhainer, sen.

Seventh. The next pastor chosen by the congregation was in the person of Rev. John P. Hecht, who entered upon his duties in 1808, and continued until about the year A.D. 1814.

Eighth. Next was elected Rev. Henry Geisenhainer, who for several years dispensed the Word of Life, from April 15th, 1814, when he was removed from time to eternity.

Ninth. In April, 1821, his brother Frederick Wm. Geisenhainer, sen., succeeded him, and

Tenth. In 1823, Frederick Wm. Geisenhainer, jr., son of the former Frederick William, was elected his successor, who officiated until 1827.

Eleventh. July, 1827, Rev. Jacob Wampole became pastor, who faithfully served this congregation until April, 1834, when the pastorate being too large for one man, was divided, and he taking the part lying across the Schuylkill, in Chester county, relinquished this part of the charge.

Twelfth. Rev. J. W. Richards was chosen in May of the same year shepherd of this flock, which relation he sustained for two years, when he accepted a call from the Lutheran Church in Germantown.

Thirteenth. On the 4th of April, 1836, the Rev. Jacob Wampole was re-called to the pastorship of this congregation, vacated by Rev. T. W. Richards's removal.

He was not permitted to labor long in this charge. He closed his labors upon earth, and entered upon the reward of the righteous on the third day of January, 1838, making the fourth of the watchmen who fell at their post of duty in this venerable sanctuary of the Most High.

Fourteenth. In the same year of Mr. Wampole's decease, the Rev. Henry S. Miller was chosen by the congregation as his successor, who served for fourteen years.

Fifteenth. In August, 1852, the Rev. G. A. Wenzel entered upon his duties as pastor of this church. During his ministry, the new church edifice was built, and with him closes the history of the ministers who here officiated as pastors.

And now to the good and blessed object for which it has been repaired and refitted, let it solemnly be devoted, in the name of the Father, the Son, and the Holy Ghost. AMEN.

To

MY DEAR BROTHER IN CHRIST, AND FOR NEAR HALF A CENTURY A FRIEND,

CHRISTIAN FREDERICK CRUSÉ.

In Memory of

COUNTLESS HOURS OF SWEET CONVERSE ON "THINGS PERTAINING TO THE KINGDOM,"

AND IN TESTIMONY OF WISDOM AND LEARNING, ALIKE MEEK AND PROFOUND,

DISCLOSED ONLY IN SUCH HOURS,

The Following Sermon is Affectionately Inscribed.

W. A. M.

SERMON.

REVELATION xix. 10.

The Testimony of Jesus is the Spirit of prophecy.

AMONG the various feelings of this occasion, a very lively one, I am sure, is a grateful approbation of the pious zeal which has not suffered this venerable sanctuary to become only a venerable ruin. They to whom we owe it deserve our cordial thanks. By many it would have been thought a needless undertaking, or one, at most, of mere sentiment; and in the spirit of our utilitarian times, these deserted walls might have been left to the ordinary fate of the useless and the old. The winds of heaven had unroofed them. If that was not a warrant, it might have served as an excuse for resigning them to the desolation which the hand of Providence itself had already begun. But you desired no excuse. The old church was too dear and hallowed to be a church no more. Consecrated by the worship of your fathers and their fathers' fathers, vocal so long with their prayer and praise, you would not allow it to moulder in decay, as if telling the decay also of their memories in your hearts. The storm which laid bare these sacred precincts was only your summons to repair their wastes, and to hand them over to your offspring unspoiled, to be still reverenced by them as one of the first monuments of their ancestors' faith and piety on these Western shores. I was glad to learn your intention, and to aid in procuring the means for carrying it into effect. No great amount, indeed, was required, as, very properly, you only wanted the time-honored structure to resume its original plainness and simplicity; yet it has been a work of genuine devotion, at the completion of which you have done well in calling us together to rejoice with you in opening again this ancient temple of the Lord.

Its first opening was in the beginning of this same month of September, one hundred and seventeen years ago, when the congregation left the barn in which they had been worshipping, and held their first service here. Since then, how many assemblies of worshippers, and among them how many whose names we trace in our family Bibles, have entered and passed away from these walls! What happy Sunday gatherings of parents and children—children in their turn becoming parents, and bringing their children to the same altar—generation after generation of families, whose lineage we should find in the baptismal records of the church. During that period, too, what changes have happened in the history of the country. Could a representative of each of the successive generations appear before us, and tell the tale of his times, with what lively annals should we be entertained—what interesting stories of character and anecdotes of our sires, justifying our resolution that this endeared memento of them shall stand, both for the church's and the country's sake. Some of these reminiscences you might expect me to call up in my present discourse, especially those relating to the men and things of this old sanctuary in its earlier days; but I must leave that to others of my brethren present, better furnished for the purpose than myself. For my own share in these services, I have chosen another, but not an irrelevant theme

—one not alien from the associations of this church, but intimately belonging to the most sacred of those associations —"The Testimony of Jesus, the Spirit of prophecy." For what is the thought which imparts the highest sacredness to this place, but that the testimony of Jesus has here been proclaimed for more than a century of years, with every opening week since He first stood here, who bore that testimony in his words and deeds alike. A true prophet of the gospel was he. To testify of Jesus, and win souls to Him, was what brought him from his dear fatherland, to this stranger and then almost wilderness land. "We are ambassadors for Christ," was the first text with which he opened his mouth. What a faithful ambassador he was, how carefully he delivered his Sovereign's instructions, how affectionately he besought his hearers to be reconciled to God, how diligently he discharged his ministry, with what simplicity and godly sincerity, publicly, and from house to house, instant in season and out of season, and how largely the Lord gave him to see the fruits of his toil, is known to all acquainted with the interesting story of his life, and may be read more in detail in the printed documents of the day.* To these a great deal might be added from the early history of the Lutheran Church in this country, which has always acknowledged him as her founder. Her members of the present day, nor they alone, assent to his epitaph on the marble here — *Qualis et quantus fuerit, secula futura,*

---

* The reports which he made of his services, in his journals sent home to the Mission-House at Halle, in Germany. It was in honor of the founder of that mission, his friend and patron, AUGUSTUS HERMANUS FRANCKE, that he gave this, his first church, the name Augustus. One of the thick quarto volumes of the *Hallische Nachrichten* is in great part made up of the reports of the "Missionary Muhlenberg."

sine lapide, non ignorabunt—" What he was, posterity without this stone will know." His best fame is that which will endure beyond the posterity of earth—a devoted missionary of Christ—a true prophet of the testimony. For a sermon, then, at his grave, my text has not been mischosen. I have taken it, however, not for the purpose of a formal discussion of it, but only as a basis and connecting link of what I shall have to say.

It is in the testimony of Jesus—that is, the testimony to Him—the declaration of all that is revealed concerning Him ; and in that testimony forming the spirit, the life, the soul of prophesying (using the word in its comprehensive sense of preaching, earnest discoursing), the identity of the preacher's office, in all times and places, consists. In this the evangelist of to-day is one with the prophets since the world began.

The prophets of the Old Testament spake indeed of other things ; they rehearsed the rise and fall of empires, chiefly the fortunes of Jerusalem, as manifesting the government of the One Ruler of nations ; but, amid all, and as the supreme event for which all political changes and national revolutions were preparing the way, they saw the advent of the Lord's Anointed. His glory, discerned through the mists of intervening ages, was the rapt vision of their sight, His name the ecstasy of their songs. Thus it was through the series of the greater and the minor prophets, till, after a lapse of centuries, during which no inspired sounds were heard, the archangel prophet broke the silence : " His name shall be called Jesus, and of His kingdom there shall be no end." Then came the voice on the banks of the Jordan—Behold the Lamb of God ; and that followed immediately by the Prophet of prophets, prophesying of Himself, speaking as never man spake, and then handing over the testimony to His apostles. "Ye shall be witnesses of Me," were His last parting words, " in Judea and Samaria, and to the utmost ends of the earth.* Noble witnesses they were after that the Holy Ghost had come upon them, and given them the tongues of fire for uttering the testimony in words of light and flame, which then flashed in upon men's minds, and kindled their hearts new-born with the truth. Of their preachings, that was the one and never exhausted text—Jesus, the Christ. What else had St. Peter to say? he who once faltered in the testimony, but was afterwards bold as a lion with its spirit. Of John and the others, what was their subject and ever-recurring refrain but the Name for which they were only too happy to suffer, and by their scourgings and dungeons were only moved to tell out more clear. Stephen proclaims it in the synagogue of the

---

* The witnessing for Christ by the apostles and first preachers, among people to whom they first made Him known, would consist more of statements of the facts of His life, and of His person and offices, than is now necessary in congregations familiar with the gospel. Still, the preaching of Christ is, in all ages, substantially the same. From knowing Him historically men are to be enlightened with a saving knowledge of Him by faith, in order to which He is continually to be set before them, as revealed in the narratives and teachings of the New Testament. To lead men to behold Jesus Christ in His essential nature, and in His relations to them, and in theirs to Him, is the great object of the Christian preacher. This never fails to supply him with a boundless variety of theme. He will know how to make each of his sermons, whether declaratory, doctrinal, ethical, or hortatory, a testimony of Jesus, and the more simply and directly he does that, the more he will do the true work of an evangelist. The peculiar work of the preachers of the first age, was to lay broad and sure the historic basis of Christianity. Preachers of every age are to develop the unsearchable riches of Christ, of which age after age knows more and more unto the end.

In the sermon, by the testimony of Jesus, I understand the testimony *to* or *for* Jesus. It may also mean Jesus's testimony; the testimony which He declared of the Father and of Himself, the whole revelation which he came to make—but this is included in all right testimony *to* or *for* Him.

adversaries, ceases not amid the shower of stones, and with his last breath cries, " I see Jesus standing at the right hand of God." The storm of persecution which then arose was the commission of those who fled before it, to go everywhere preaching the Christ. And Paul—Paul, he whom Jesus chose to be the great exponent of Himself, to be a preacher after His own heart, on whom was concentrated more than all the gifts of the rest of the apostolic college, what His testimony to His Lord was—how he bestowed upon it the learning, and knowledge, and eloquence, and reasoning, which would have made him great on any other theme, how it was the one actuating spirit of his heart and mind and soul ; to see that you must read the greater part of the book of the Acts, and his Epistles through and through, glowing in every line with the love of Christ constraining Him, knowing nothing but Christ and Him crucified, laboring under a sense of the unsearchable riches of Christ, " counting all things as dross for the excellency of the knowledge of Christ Jesus His Lord." Their testimony the apostles transmitted to their successors in the hosts of evangelists, bearing it to every part of the world. Wherever they went, whoever were their hearers, peasants or princes, of whatever nation, kindred, or people, or tongue, their word was one and the same—salvation through the Crucified. Their converts learned that first and last. In their worshipping assemblies we read, they sang hymns to Christ as to God. In their persecutions for the faith, they looked to no other support than that one Name, the subject of their converse in dens and caves of the earth, their one encouragement to be faithful unto death. Martyrs, you know, means witnesses—men bearing their testimony. Unchanged it was heard from amidst the flames. Another and another

Stephen of the noble army died with the prayer—" Lord Jesus, receive my spirit." That Name of might was the secret of their power, as the moral conquerors of the world. Immovable in its strength, they felt themselves the Hosts of the Lord. Their enemies joined their ranks. The Jerichos of Heathendom fell before the blasts of their trumpets, and the kingdoms of the world, in an outward submission to the cross, at least, became the kingdoms of God and of His Christ. Glorious was the triumph of the prophets, mighty the spirit of the testimony, when from its first whisper in Eden —" the seed of the woman shall bruise the serpent's head " —it persisted until it was heard in alleluias to Emmanuel through the empire of the Cæsars, and the herald of the Galilean planted his cross on the summit palace of the earth.

Meanwhile, however, a change had been coming over the evangelic office. The ministry of Jesus did not continue, according to its original institution, a simple ministry of the word. Multitudes, indeed, there were still of the primitive stamp, witnesses like Paul and John ; and these were from among the laity as well as the clergy, until the clerical office proper, or the clerical order, as it had now become, gradually assumed the character of a priesthood. Christ's ministers, besides being evangelists, pastors, and teachers, also became mediators between Him and the souls of men. Not only as His ambassadors did they announce pardon to the penitent, and point out to him the way of salvation ; they now began to dispense pardon and to negotiate salvation. They held the keys of the kingdom of heaven, and claimed to bind and unloose souls in a way of which we read nothing in Peter or Paul. Thus their office acquired an ecclesiastical worth, but lost in proportion its evangelical power. As the night of the middle ages set in, bringing with it a return to Jewish darkness, less and less was heard of the pure testimony of Jesus, and in its place were substituted sacerdotal rites and ceremonies, and sacrificial services at altars. For the celebration of these but little knowledge was necessary. The priest could exercise his functions and scarcely know a page of Holy Writ—might be an adept in his craft, yet be unable to read. Among the Greeks, as early as the sixth century, preaching was all but extinct. It was much the same with the Latins. Among the latter, those of St. Bernard are the only discourses for a long period ; at least none others are extant. In the ninth century, Charlemagne assembled all the learned men in Europe to revive the ministry of preaching. Among a thousand priests there was not one able to preach, when a book of Homilies was prepared by order of the emperor, from which the clergy might read to the people. Of course there were exceptions. In the monasteries there must have been many a holy father who loved the precious words which his pen transcribed in the manuscript he loved to adorn, who saw his Saviour in the crucifix, and spake of Him to his brethren of the cell. There must have been many a good pastor who fed his flock as he could amid that famine of the Word ; for God had then his elect, whom he would not leave to perish for lack of knowledge. Amid that well-nigh Egyptian darkness, the souls in His Israel had light in their dwellings. The testimony of Jesus could not wholly be suppressed. Here and there a prophet, in a Wickliff, a Huss, and others, with special illumination from on high, spake out. Still, speaking generally, there was an ignorance of everything concerning the way of salvation but the power of the clergy to give absolution. The poor sinner, troubled in conscience, sought peace by paying his pence at the confessional, not knowing that he could go at once to his God for pardon without money and without price. Deep and fearful was the silence of the testimony, when at length, after premonitory notes by others, it came ringing loud and clear in the trumpet tones of the monk of Wittenberg. God's hero-prophet arose to republish the gospel. His thunder-words of truth startled men into audience, and broke up the long night of the Church. "Let there be light," the decree had come from on high, "and there was light." The watchmen who had fallen asleep, woke up and assured by their great leader, mounted their watch-towers and proclaimed the morning. Songs of praise ushered in the day, telling how glad men were to hail the light and to hear the testimony of Jesus again. Once more the Apostle of the gentiles, whose doctrines had been held in abeyance, or buried under the rubbish of ecclesiastics, was heard in the Apostle of the Reformation. As the former, with the sword of the spirit, had pierced to the heart the old Roman world; so the latter, wielding the same weapon, struck terror into the second Rome, and set the captive nations free from her chains, even by "the foolishness of preaching." Of the "great company of preachers," then, when the Lord again gave the Word, to be uttered with the power of the Lord, Luther was the foremost. The arch-evangelist of the day, he did more than any other to restore the Christian ministry to its primitive office as a ministry of the word. As he had struck the most effectual blow at the priesthood, so he did the most to bring back the preacherhood. Nor did he only preach and argue and write, and give to the people the word of God in their mother tongue, in that noblest of all the modern versions of the Bible, next to our own; like the inspired prophets of old, he poured out his prophesyings also in song. Gloriously did he sing forth his Gospel, according the hearts of the multitude to his own, in choral strains speeding on the truth in bursts of harmony over the land. In glowing outpourings of the Gospel muse, the testimony of Jesus was borne with new power in the hymns of the Reformation. They stirred hearts then, as they stir them still. They have not worn out ; multiplied, in age after age, by the minstrels of a nation ever vocal in song, full of the richest and sweetest thoughts of the love of God in Christ, a repository of pure theology in melodious devotion, they are the peculiar treasure of the Lutheran Church, making her the Choral Church of Christendom.

In the lapse of years missionary successors of the Reformation preachers came here with their gospel doctrines and hymns. Here they took up the burden of their prophesyings, the ministers in their sermons, and the people with them in their songs. With this as a central point they gathered congregations and erected churches ; in doing which, it may be well in these days to say, they were true to the testimony as maintained in the old standard of their fathers. They were evangelical, not rationalizing, half-sceptical protestants. Neology had not shed its bewildering light. And that you, my brethren, do not desire to walk in that light, I take to be in part the meaning of your preserving this ancient pile. You declare by this act, that you adhere to the creed of your patriarch and his immediate followers. This landmark which they set you say shall not be removed, but shall stand as a witness of what they believed and taught, and is received and loved by their children. You will have this old Augustus Church still to stand in its antique form, beside your new sanctuary bearing the same name, to remind the minister and congregation, that the old, not the new theology, is the true testimony of Jesus. Therefore the more cheerfully do I unite in this celebration, happy thus to show myself one with you in those great articles of the faith, in which your communion, and that in which I am a minister, are entirely agreed. Our separation is not in that of doctrine. Between the Church of England and the Lutheran Church, the most intimate relations existed ever since the time they were allies in their common battle against Rome. For the last half century or upwards, from various causes, there has been more estrangement, of which, however, there was nothing at the time of the first Lutherans and Episcopalians in this country.* Their

* In an article, by Professor Stoever, in the Evangelical Review, Gettysburg, Penn., April, 1856, there are the following statements:—

"In the year 1763, we find the Rev. Messrs. Peters and Ingliss, of the Episcopal Church, Philadelphia, present at the Synodical meeting of our Church."

"At a meeting of the Synod of North Carolina, in the year 1821, a committee of the Episcopalian Church was in attendance for the purpose of conferring on some plan by which friendly relations might be maintained between the two Churches; the result of this interview was, that any Lutheran minister should be entitled to a seat in the Episcopal Convention of North Carolina, with the privilege of voting upon all subjects that did not specially appertain to the Episcopal Church, and vice versa."

The Rev. Dr. Kunze, an eminent theologian of the Lutheran Church, and Professor of the German Language and Literature in Columbia College, New York, in the preface to a volume of sermons, published in 1797, gives an historical sketch of the intimate relations of the English and Lutheran Churches, after which he says:—"I have these twenty-four years, i. e. as long as I have instructed students of divinity for my church, held this and no other language to them, and it was in consequence of this subsisting union, that the Evangelical Lutheran Consistory, held at Rhinebeck, N. Y., on the first of September, 1797, adopted the following resolution: 'That on account of the intimate connexion existing between the English Episcopal and the Lutheran Churches, and the identity of their doctrine and near alliance of their church discipline, this Consistory will never acknowledge a newly erected Lutheran Church, merely English, in places where the members may partake of the services of the said English Episcopal Church.' " The fact is

mutual friendly attitude appears from many facts that might
be stated; a significant one is, that your patriarch was pleased
to have one of his sons in the ministry of the Church of England. From private family tradition I could say much of his
affection for the English Lutheran, as he would sometimes
call the Episcopal church. When Zion, a German Lutheran
church in Philadelphia, was consecrated in the year 1769,
"on the second day of the solemnities, the services were
according to the liturgy of the Church of England, and a sermon was preached by the Rev. Dr. Peters, a clergyman of that
church. Several other Episcopal ministers were present on
the occasion, at the conclusion of which, the Rector Muhlenberg, who had delivered the sermon on the first day, returned
thanks to the assembled congregation, and in the name of the
corporation of Zion church adverted to the many kind proofs of
sympathy they had received during the three years in which
they had worshipped in a building belonging to the Episcopalians, and the additional gratification they had just experi-
enced in the services conducted by their Episcopal brethren."

Between Bishop White, the patriarch of the American
Episcopal Church, and your patriarch—I had almost said
your Bishop, he was so in affection and influence, if not in
authority—there existed a most cordial intimacy which, in
my younger days, I often heard the Bishop refer to, repeating
anecdotes showing the Episcopal sympathies of his Lutheran
friend and brother. That good and truly great man, it is my
privilege to say, was my spiritual father, in nearer than mere
ecclesiastical bonds. Well do I recollect (you will pardon
this little egotism) the smile with which he said to me, after

well known that the Society of the Church of England for "Propagating the Gospel in foreign parts," until within comparatively recent years, often employed
Lutheran missionaries, without requiring from them Episcopal ordination.

my first ordination at his hands, "The shade of your great-grandfather has not frowned, I am sure, on what we have done to-day;" nor, let me now add, does the shade of my dear spiritual father frown upon his son, in a Lutheran pulpit to-day.

Had the temper and spirit of moderation of those good men generally prevailed in our two communions, we should have found some way of coming together ere this, instead of remaining apart as we now do, adding to the unhappy divisions of the Christian world. No others of the reformed bodies ought rather to be one, for no others have so much in common. In all the great matters of the testimony, we are one. We adhere to the ancient and universal creeds often found in your old Lutheran bibles as well as in our prayer-books. We have the same theological doctrines, seeing that your Augsburg Confession was the basis of our XXXIX Articles, which confession, Bishop Bull, one of the great lights of the Church of England, after stating the fact that our articles were framed on it, pronounces "the noblest symbol of the Reformed Churches."

In the orders of the ministry we differ, though there we might practically agree, were your ministry constituted as it is in the Lutheran churches of some of the northern countries of Europe. We both have the spirit of ministerial and church order. In the administration of the sacraments we are nearly alike, and in their doctrine also, as it is now received by the majorities in both our communions, and where the same diversities of views on the subject are found; high and low Churchmen, high and low Lutherans tolerating one another in the comprehensiveness of the faith. We both have the rite of confirmation as a proper complement of infant baptism. With us it is administered only by the Bishop;

in the case, however, of any one coming into our Church, who had been confirmed by a Lutheran clergyman, Bishop White did not think it necessary to repeat the rite. Together we observe the seasons of the church-year, having the same round of gospels and epistles for the Sundays, festivals, and fasts. In this as well as in other things, our liturgies agree, both having been derived from the same sources.

True, we have adhered more constantly to our Liturgy—and would it not have been well (allow me to ask, as I do in the most brotherly spirit) if you also had adhered more constantly to yours—not to the exclusion of free prayer, but together with that, according to the practice of all the continental churches long after the Reformation, and to a great extent now, as also, I believe, in many of your congregations.

It is not simply from partiality for that to which I am accustomed, that I think a scriptural and unchanging service book greatly becomes a church, adoring her unchanging Lord. It secures the uniformity of her worship, and so manifests its unity in all her congregations. The Liturgy is her perpetual testimony of Jesus.* It is a living creed, which, more than any dogmatic formulas, keeps alive the truth in the hearts and minds of the worshippers. Generation after generation takes it up unchanged. The Glorias and Litanies, uttered by our remotest ancestors, we repeat to-day, confident they will be the Glorias and Litanies of the ages to come—the present church thus symbolizing and feeling her identity with the future and the past. Never, says Mr. Cecil, do I enter one of our old cathedrals without being

* The English Liturgy is a grand witness for the objective faith of the whole church, while the Lutheran Hymns are a rich expression of the subjective faiths of individual believers. But each, of course, is more or less of the other.

deeply impressed with the thought, that for ages these vaults have resounded with the acclaim—Thou art the King of Glory, O Christ!

Further, let me express my conviction (you will accord me the privilege of years) of the value of a Liturgy as a safeguard of the truth and a protection against lapsing into error. Without such inclosure, I cannot tell how far I might have been enticed by the subtleties of German rationalistic criticism, and of science falsely so-called, during a period of my ministry, peculiarly exposed to such danger. However it may be with others, I feel it a subject of devout gratitude to God that in the orderings of His providence my lot has been cast in a church, where I must needs confess " the Faith once delivered to the saints" —where it has not been left to my choice whether or not I should make the catholic ascription of glory to the Father, and to the Son, and to the Holy Ghost—where it has not been optional with me or my congregation, in offering our prayers, to plead the name of the One mediator between God and man. Thankful am I that it did not rest with me to read or not as I pleased a set portion of God's Word to the people. Blessed constraint, if such it was, that whatever was the defect of my own discourses, the testimony of Jesus was proclaimed in the lessons, the psalms, the creeds, and the prayers, so that the flock never went away unfed with the bread of life.

In this view of the subject, it is not mere Episcopalianism to maintain that in venerating our Liturgy we have done better than the reformed churches which have laid theirs aside. That cannot be, since, in all their important parts, the Liturgies are a common heritage from the early church. If you are offended by any among us, talking of *our* Te Deum, *our* Gloria in excelsis, you should excuse the ignorance occasioned by the disuse of those old treasures, and show by a practical appreciation of them that they are yours as much as ours.

Thus we see there are many considerations which should foster our sympathies as kindred communions. They show us how nearly we approximate, and must sometimes prompt the desire that we might go on from proximity to union. And why not union? These walls of division between us, are certainly nothing desirable in themselves. They present the church in her outward aspect in sad contrast to her interior and real unity. For a while, perhaps, they must stand. The time for their removal may not have come. If it be His will, the Lord will bring it about in His own day. In the meanwhile, our distinctive principles, however conscientiously we maintain them, need be no barrier to a union of hearts. For no reason should they stand in the way of brotherly love and mutual good will. The unity of the Spirit and the bond of peace, lie deep within, and beyond the reach of outward disturbance. And yet can there be no advance towards outward union? Can there not be some demonstration of our oneness, so far as we are one, which might be seen and known of all men. I dare to think there might. We are united in the testimony of Jesus. We of the clergy (it is the clergy who must be foremost in any efforts for union) are one as prophets of that Testimony. It is the one spirit of our prophesyings. In other words, we are all preachers of the gospel. In that regard our office is the same. Whether Lutherans or Episcopalians we preach the gospel, and we have no difference of opinion as to what the gospel is. We are equally ambassadors for Christ, praying men for His sake to be reconciled to God. In this we have a common office; but at the same time we have another office, which is not common to us, and that is our office as ministers of our respective churches. Christ-ward, our office is the same; church-ward, it is diverse. As clergymen we have a twofold character—an evangelical and ecclesiastical character. It is in the former character, without at all entrenching upon the latter, that we might make mutual advances. In our capacity as preachers, we might recognise one another, not merely in private sentiment and feeling, but openly and officially. While in our church capacity we can minister acceptably only to our own congregations, what should hinder our appearing before one another's congregations, in our common and evangelical capacity as preachers of the Lord Jesus Christ? Making this distinction, there might be union, so far, between us, and that without the least relinquishment, on either side, of any principle of our respective communions. Would that it might be brought about and regulated by some mutual and formal act of consent.

But I am not here to propose anything. I speak with no authority. I only avail myself of the opportunity for the setting forth of views which of late years have been very clear to my mind, and which seem to me to present a ground of union not only between our two bodies (who, indeed, should be the first to recognise and act upon it), but among all the reformed churches which adhere to their confessions. Through the preacherhood let them exhibit their substantial agreement. Let their variously constituted ministries, government, and order, be upheld as strictly as they please, while that which they have in common is declared with equal zeal. Their specific *differentia* need not interfere with their generic sameness; only in asserting the *species*, let not the *genus* be ignored, but be practically proclaimed. It is high time for such a demonstration. Justice to ourselves, to the gospel, to the glory of our Lord, demands it. Men take our separations as signs of so many creeds. Let us teach them better. Let us show them that these are only signs of so many opinions subordinate to the one creed—only so many species of one genus. Let us show them that the protestantism of the Reformation is not just the aggregation of schisms denounced by Rome, nor of discordant superstitions scorned by infidelity. Let us show them that it has one heart and one mind in all things requisite to salvation, that it drops not one of the catholic verities, that it owns one Lord, one Faith, one Baptism, one God and Father of All—the whole included in the Testimony of Jesus.

And I do believe, this most desirable demonstration would come to pass, if only the Testimony were, to the extent in which it ought to be, the spirit of our prophesyings. It is in the main, but it should be vastly more. Here we are lacking. Here we are at fault. I say this not of one church more than of another. It may be predicated of some rather than of others, but it attaches in different degrees to us all. The reason why the voice of a united preacherhood might not be welcomed in all our pulpits, is that the great truths which it would proclaim—the testimony in which we are all agreed—is not enough the theme of our discoursings. We are too fond of testifying of our peculiar doctrines, our favorite dogmas, our own systems and institutions, of ourselves disguised from ourselves, under cover of zeal for the truth. In plainer language, we all have too much of the spirit of sect. It is that which, far more than we are aware, stimulates our zeal. It is the Trumpet of the Lord, which we fain think we are so glad to sound or to hear—the sweet, silver trumpets of the blessed gospel—aye, but it is when their notes have the Lutheran, or the Episcopal, or the Presbyterian tone, that they have their highest charm. We fondly love our own theologic or ecclesiastic melodies, and believing them to be only the pure music of Zion, we claim that all the inhabitants of Zion should love them as well. It is natural —but rather carnal than spiritual—more of the old man than the new. It is akin to the spirit of the Jews in Jeremiah's days. Each pointing to his own ecclesiastical structure, cries, Like them, the Temple of the Lord, the Temple of the Lord are these. See, says one, the glory of this Temple of ours—so ancient, so grand and stately without, and within, having "all things made after the pattern of things shown in the Mount." See, says another, *our* beautiful sanctuary, our goodly order, our sound doctrine, our primitive simplicity. But mark, cries a third, how God blesses our ministrations—see what converts we make—and what holy lives our people lead. Go round about *our* Zion, calls another and another, mark well her bulwarks and the towers thereof, and say whether this be not the very city of God." No wonder that each prophet, contrary to the proverb, is most popular at home (men always loving to hear themselves bepraised) and speaks with less acceptance abroad. No wonder, too, that those without are distracted by the opposite calls, "Lo here," and "lo there," and bid us first settle among ourselves which is the Temple of the Lord, ere we are so urgent for them to come in. Yes, it is natural. It has always been so. "I am of Paul—I of Apollos—I of Cephas," began in the apostles' times. It was the bane of the churches immediately upon the reformation, in the hot strifes which so unhappily estranged foremost men in that gospel revolution. How rife, alas! in our own land, I need not say, and in the best of men. Scarce anywhere does the flame of religious zeal burn vigorously, but with marked alloy of this earthly fire. "The times of this ignorance God winked at, but now commandeth his people everywhere to repent," to confess the sin of the bigotry, the sectarian spirit, and narrow-heartedness which have made such havoc in the household of faith, to turn to Him, and seek, not their glory, but His, first and alone. Not the temple of the Lord, be now the cry, but the Lord of the temple, the Lord of all the temples where His name is proclaimed and adored. Concordant then will be the voices of the evangelists, with no dissonance of party sounds, and welcomed everywhere in Zion. No longer will men be distracted by conflicting testimony; for when we point to the temple's Lord, we shall all point one way—not, lo! here, or lo! there, but to Christ all and in all. From the goodly fellowship of the prophets, now again in these latter days, as once from the "glorious choir of the apostles," will go forth clear and distinct the theme, varied in endless descant for every genius and every character of mind, yet unchanged—the exhaustless theme, the same borne on "the ages all along:" Jesus Christ, the first and the last, the same yesterday, to-day, and for ever; Jesus Christ, the root and offspring of David, the Bright and Morning Star; the Only begotten of the Father, full of grace and truth; the Desire of all nations; the First-born among many brethren; the Author and Finisher of our faith; the Shepherd and Bishop of our souls; the Lamb of God, taking away the sin of the world; the Prophet, Priest, and King; the Lord our right-eousness; the Crown of glory and Diadem of beauty unto His people; the Judge of the quick and the dead; King of kings and Lord of lords; God over all, blessed for evermore.

33

Oh, in this chorus of the testimony of Jesus, lift we up, dear brethren of every name, lift we up our voices anew, acknowledging and affectioning all whom the Spirit of the Lord attunes to its strains, joying to unite with them, heart with heart, and voice with voice, pouring forth a grander than the harmony of the spheres, till with one overpowering acclaim, it fill the holy church throughout the world, charming all ears that can hear, and constraining everywhere the confession, that JESUS CHRIST IS LORD, TO THE GLORY OF GOD THE FATHER.

With the love of Him, and with love to one another in Him, may our hearts be knit in the fellowship of the Holy Ghost. Then, whatever outward union we may lack, in that heart of true union we shall be one. The notes of our difference will be scarce heard in the blessed concord. Our partition walls will sink beneath the range of our vision, as we look up towards the walls of the city on the everlasting hills. In the meanwhile, the Lord, we may be sure, is constructing that kingdom of His, which will not fail to be at unity with itself: whether in any outward organization, in a happy future of our world, we cannot foretell, but certainly, in His temple of living stones, like that of old, reared without the sound of axe or hammer, without the noise of human contrivance, much less of human strife—that Everlasting Temple of which Jesus Christ is the corner-stone elect and precious. On that foundation may we be builded. In that structure may we be set among the living stones. For that let our lives now be a living testimony of Jesus, confessing Him, presenting our souls and bodies to Him a living sacrifice, and so following those of our fathers, who in their day and generation bore their testimony to Him within these walls. They have passed away for their places within

3

those other walls which never waste, of crystal and gold, and all manner of precious stones. In our turn we shall pass away. Shall it be to *our* places with them, in the New Jerusalem? Shall it be to join our voices with theirs in the everlasting testimony of the elect: " Unto Him that hath loved us, and washed us from our sins in His own blood, be all glory and dominion evermore."

So grant it, O Father, for the sake of Thy Son, by the Holy Ghost: to Whom be glory, as it was in the beginning, is now, and ever shall be, world without end. Amen.

POSTSCRIPT.

[*The Committee who requested the publication of the Sermon have no knowledge of the contents of this Postscript, which may or may not meet their approbation. I presume on their indulgence in attaching to the Sermon, what is meant more particularly for members of my own communion.*]

KNOWING that many of my Episcopal brethren will have a radical objection to any views towards union, which acknowledge men as preachers who are without Episcopal ordination, I have thought well to append an answer to this objection, respectfully submitted to their consideration.

There is no instance in the New Testament of any one after the apostles being ordained to preach the gospel. The apostles were so ordained by Christ, but it nowhere appears that they ordained others—I mean as preachers. They did not themselves begin to preach immediately upon their commission by Christ, but waited, according to His command, until they were endued with power from on high. On the day of Pentecost they were so endued. "Cloven tongues like as of fire sat upon each of them, and they began to speak with tongues as the Spirit gave them utterance." This, however, is said not of the twelve alone, but of the whole assembly of whom we read immediately before, that "they were all assembled with one accord in one place." On each of that company of disciples alighted the tongue of fire ; each began to speak as the Spirit gave him utterance. Though we need not construe the "all" so strictly, yet it certainly implies that more than the apostles were the subjects of the miracle. As they "spake of the wonderful works of God," their utterances were, probably, as some think, a united burst of praise ;* but they must have been more or less also of the nature of preaching :

* See Baumgarten's Apostolic History, *in loco*, and the former part of the work generally for an able elucidation of the main point here discussed.

for St. Peter immediately proceeds to say that then was fulfilled the prediction of the prophet Joel, of an outpouring
of the Spirit, whereby all should prophesy.* Accordingly,
on Whitsunday we use the psalm in which it is said,
"The Lord gave the company of the preachers." Foremost
among them were the apostles; but soon after we find
Stephen preaching, to which we have no account of his
being appointed by the apostles. He was one of the seven
set by them over the daily charitable ministrations of the
church, in order that they might be relieved from serving tables, and give themselves wholly to the ministry
of the word. But Stephen, in accepting the ministry
of the table, had no idea of laying aside the ministry
of the word, which he, together with the apostles, had
received of the Holy Ghost. We read that he was a man
"full of the Holy Ghost and wisdom," "full of faith and
power, and that he did great wonders and miracles among
the people;" and further, that " the wisdom and the Spirit
with which he spake, his adversaries could not resist;"
and we know how he preached with his dying breath.
Thus, the first martyr appears as the first preacher of the
gospel after the apostles, but not ordained by them—not
commissioned by any human instrumentality—no successor
in office of the apostles. The only office which they gave
him was one which they declined to hold.

Next appears (Acts viii. 4) another great company of preachers. Whence did they get their commission? In the persecution which began with the murder of Stephen. "Then they
that were scattered abroad went everywhere preaching the
word." The apostles remained in Jerusalem firm at their posts
amid the rising violence, feeling that if their cause was aban-
doned there all hope for it in Judea was gone. But the gospel
could not be confined to Jerusalem; it must go on its errand

* "Your handmaidens and daughters shall prophesy," says the text. But
St. Paul suffers not a woman to speak in the church. If that was a primitive
canon, the sphere of the female prophetesses or preachers might have been their
own households, or on other occasions than public assemblies of the church.

to " Samaria and the ends of the world." And who should carry it thither but they who had been charged to do so by the Lord himself in His parting words to them ? But these as yet make the holy city the bounds of their mission. What wider missions they afterwards entered upon we are not informed in the inspired records, but gather only from tradition. In the meanwhile, do they appoint their delegates for carrying the word beyond Jerusalem ? We read not of it. We are not told of their laying their hands on evangelists, as they had done on the ministers of the table. Evangelists were already made in men who knew the power of the gospel, and who, from the abundance of the heart with which the mouth speaketh, were ready when the occasion came to publish it. The thunders of the storm which drove them from Jerusalem was their summons to set out on their work. It will be said they had the approbation of the apostles. Undoubtedly they had—approbation, of course. We cannot imagine these missionaries of the dispersion first waiting upon the twelve for leave, while they were scattered abroad, to go " everywhere preaching the word." Among them was Philip, who had been ordained to the same service as Stephen, and who, with Stephen, felt that he had that higher service, in which we find him engaged in one of the chief cities of Samaria, the region in which the Lord had enjoined His apostles to be His witnesses. There Philip is the apostle, there he preaches the gospel, makes converts, baptizes, and causes great joy in the city. An unordained missionary founds the church in Samaria. Hearing of it, the apostles in Jerusalem sent two of their number to signify their approval of Philip's work, and especially to recognise the new converts, by exercising their apostolic prerogative of conferring upon them the extraordinary gifts of the Holy Ghost.* In doing this, they put the Samaritan believers on a level with the believers in Jerusalem, and so declared them fellow-members of one church. Philip had further

---

* Simon could not have seen and coveted *ordinary* gifts of the Holy Ghost.

sanction of his ministry in the voice of an angel sending
him to the Ethiopian nobleman, to whom he preaches Christ,
baptizes him, and leaves him to go on his way rejoicing to
his home in the remotest parts of the then known world.
There, tradition tells us, he was the means of widely diffus-
ing the gospel. If so, it was not in virtue of any laying on
of hands for the purpose. Indeed, for no purpose were
hands laid on the eunuch after his baptism. Neither confirmed nor ordained, his knowing Christ was his warrant for
proclaiming Him to his countrymen.

From the eleventh chapter of the Acts, we find that some of
these preachers of the dispersion had gone as far as Antioch,
where, through their ministry, a great number believed and
turned to the Lord. Tidings of the gospel in the third city
of the Roman empire was great news for the church at
Jerusalem, where the twelve still tarried. Forthwith they
despatch a brother to Antioch with their salutations. It is
not one of their own number that goes, and with apostolic
powers, to ratify the new church. Barnabas, the Son of
Consolation, we may imagine was eager for an embassy of
fellowship and brotherly love. When he came, we read of
his performing no official acts, but only that " he was glad
when he saw the grace of God, and exhorted them all
that with purpose of heart they should cleave unto the
Lord." Thinking that one like Paul was needed for such a
field of labor, he looked him up, and brought him to Antioch,
where they two continued a year in building up the church,
the members of which were first called Christians, and the
foundations of which were laid by those whom we should
now call, missionary laymen.

The theory, then, that Christ, at His ascension, committed
all authority to preach the gospel only to His apostles, and
to those to whom they formally transmitted that authority,
and through whom, as their successors, He would be with
the apostles to the end of the world—that He thus established
an order of preachers never to be entered by any outside
of such a transmitted succession—cannot be maintained in

view of such facts from Scripture as those just adduced. It is at variance, too, with the preaching of St. Paul himself. He began without any authority from the twelve. For a while they did not even know him. True, he had his commission immediately from the Lord; but if the Lord had established a fixed and indispensable order for the propagation of His gospel (as is contended), why was not Paul required to conform to it? Of the fact of his commission immediately by Christ, no one had any evidence but himself. Why was he not directed to go to Jerusalem for ordination by the twelve, instead of being only sent to Ananias (of whom we read nowhere else) for baptism, and so be recognised by, and have the sanction of the central authority of the church. So far from that, he acted quite independently of the apostolic college. He had very little connexion with it through the whole of his ministry. There is great significance in the "divine irregularity," as Dr. Schaff calls it, of St. Paul's mission. He gloried that he had received his apostleship not from man, but from God; and for the evidence of it, he told his converts, "Ye are the seals of mine apostleship in the Lord."

But did not St. Paul himself ordain men? Yes—men to be Bishops and Elders. The twelve ordained the seven, whom we call deacons, though the record does not call them so. St. James seems to have presided in the first council, and probably had church jurisdiction in Jerusalem. Everything of that kind which we read of in the Acts and Epistles relates to the matter of church government, order, discipline, of which I am now saying nothing. I confine myself to the single point, that we find no examples in the New Testament of the formal investment of men, after the apostles, with the office of preacher.* Indeed, it could hardly be otherwise. The preachers of the New Testament take the place of the prophets of the Old Testament, and these latter had no external commission. They belonged

* The laying of hands on Barnabas and Saul, Acts. xiii. 3, was at their appointment to a special mission, and that was by unordained men.

to no line of succession. They were outside of the priesthood. " Holy men of old spake as they were moved by the Holy Ghost." Such holy men could not have ceased with the incoming of the gospel, under which the Holy Ghost is given more abundantly. We read, " He gave first apostles, secondarily prophets." Again, the church is " built on the foundation of the apostles and prophets," that is the apostles' and prophets' foundation —that on which they built—hence these must be prophets of the evangelical, not of the legal dispensation. In the apostolic church prophecy was one of the gifts of the Holy Ghost, and that which had been largely bestowed (according to St. Peter's interpretation of Joel, to which we have already referred), on the day of Pentecost, when Moses's wish that " all the Lord's people were prophets" was, so far as they were qualified, fulfilled.

All this, it may be replied, is very true, but no argument can thence be drawn for unordained preachers now. Those times were original and peculiar. The church was just coming into being ; order was not yet established. The work of the church was not yet distributed. The elements of, but not organization itself existed. For the while believers generally might be preachers, especially when the Spirit was so abounding, and all were glowing with their first love impelling them everywhere to tell of the great salvation. Be it so, I answer, but there the Scriptures leave us, and if they leave us without any order established as to the matter in question, then for no subsequent order can we claim scriptural obligation or precedent. We may plead antiquity (though that on the point before us is denied), expediency, ecclesiastical enactment, but not divine authority. But the church, in its earliest stages, was not without order. The community of believers in Jerusalem maintained its fellowship with the apostles, and was in due subordination to them. In the ordination of the seven there was an instance of formal induction into office, and the same might, and would have been done in the case of preachers had it been deemed necessary. Seeing it was not done we conclude it was not necessary. The omission is not to be explained by referring it to a comparatively chaotic state of the Church. It is one of the proofs that the apostles did nothing to restrict the "liberty of prophesying." Their example is precedent for all times.

"The ages of the church,* next succeeding the apostles, support, by their practice, this our interpretation of the New Testament. Among men not in holy orders may be reckoned apologists, theologians, and church historians. The learned Origen was a teacher of theology, and a preacher of the gospel, distinguished for his success in making converts,† 'at least seven years before he could be ordained deacon by the canons of the church.'‡ He was permitted by the bishops of Cesarea and Jerusalem to preach publicly in their presence. And he is defended on this ground : that "whenever there are found those qualified to benefit the brethren they were exhorted to address the people,§—of which several instances are cited. Laymen also became successful missionaries." I might refer to the practice of later ages of the Church, to the preaching lay orders of the Church of Rome, and other examples, but that would carry us too far.

Returning now to the New Testament, the prophesying of those times was inspired preaching, or as it has been defined—"Discourse flowing from the impulse and revelation of the Spirit, which not being attached to any particular office in the church, but improvised, disclosed the depths of the human heart and of the divine counsel, and thus was exceedingly effectual for the exhorting, enlightening, and consoling of believers." ‖ Answering to these we

---

* From an able pamphlet, entitled, "Lay Co-operation : a Report by a Committee of the Western District Missionary Association of the Protestant Episcopal Church in Massachusetts." The report, in the principles with which it begins its argument, agrees with my postscript, but its authors, I presume, would not assent to my practical inferences. Their object, though excellent, is a different one.

† Eusebius, Eccl. Hist. B. vi. c. 3.

‡ Bingham's Origines Eccles. B. iii. c. 10, sect. 2.

§ Eusebius, Eccl. Hist. B. vi. c 19, towards the end.

‖ Meyer as quoted by Alford on 1 Cor. xii. 10.

have prophesying now in men endowed with high gifts of nature and grace, mighty in the testimony of Jesus, full of zeal for truth and righteousness, with piercing intelligence and fervent spirit, speaking effectually to men's hearts and consciences, rightly applying the divine word to the circumstances of the times, as if it were spoken just for those times, detecting and portraying in vivid imagery the sins of nations and individuals, ever prophesying of the speedy coming of the Lord.

Such are the successors of the New Testament prophets. We contend for successors of the apostles, why not of the prophets? not, however, of any ecclesiastical lineage. The laying on of hands has nothing to do in making them.* They may minister as pastors and teachers in their respective communions, but in their higher ministry they are for all communions, and so should be received. They believe they are called of God to proclaim His word. They profess that as their warrant for proclaiming it. Surely if they are so called it is no light thing not to acknowledge them. The church which disowns them as prophets of the Lord, simply because they do not conform to her peculiar order, does so to her loss, if not at her peril.

But how shall we be satisfied that men *are* called by the Holy Spirit? I answer, in the same way that we are satisfied of it in regard to those of whom it is required in order to their ordination to our ministry. We accept their trust, their own persuasion that they are called, provided it be not contradicted by false doctrine or ungodly lives on their part. So, if there be men who trust that they are called to preach Jesus Christ, and who do truly preach Him, whose preaching God blesses by making it the means of saving souls, who lead godly, righteous, and sober lives, who stand the Saviour's test, "by their fruits ye shall know them," who can appeal to their converts, like the apostle, for the seals of their ministry, I see not how we can shut them out from ever appear-

* "We nowhere find prophets made by ordination."—Hooker. E. P. v. 78.6.

ing among us, for the one reason of their lacking episcopal orders, seeing, as I have shown, that in their characters as preachers they require no orders at all. This, indeed, applies in its full force to those who in their extraordinary gifts and evident tokens of their divine mission, have the stamp of prophets. But as prophets and preachers are of one genus, and neither depend upon ecclesiastical commission, all should be everywhere recognised and welcomed, so far as they are good men and true, and manifest the evangelical and catholic spirit which is indispensable to the profitableness of their ministry among Christians at large.

These views seem to me so radically true, that I am loth to think there is any positive barrier in our church to their acceptance. She ordains bishops, priests, and deacons, but none simply as preachers. What then becomes of men who confess to no call to be bishops, priests, or deacons, but who are right sure that they are called to be preachers? Shall they be told that they dare not be the latter, unless they are one or other of the former? That was the grand mistake which the Church of England made with the Methodist preachers. She forgot the prophetical office of the church. She did not own a preacherhood.—The preface to our ordinal forbids the exercise of priestly functions to any one not having episcopal ordination, and if preaching is necessarily a priestly function, then no man may preach among us without that qualification. But I have shown that it is not. It might seem, indeed, as if the Church wholly merged the prophetical in the priestly office, but that we cannot suppose. It would be too contrary to Scripture. It would be to confine the Spirit's gift of prophecy to limits, to the like of which it never has been confined. It would be to suffocate divine inspirations—I had almost said to smother the Holy Spirit. An Apostle *has* said, " Quench not the Spirit," which, it is remarkable for our purpose, he says in connexion with " Despise not prophesyings." The church, then, not meaning wholly to merge the prophetical office in the sacerdotal, must admit its existence outside of her ordained ministry, and admitting that, she cannot forbid its exercise within her pale. On the whole, I conclude that the language of the ordinal is irrelevant to the point in hand.

" He gave some apostles, some prophets, some evangelists, and some pastors and teachers, for the work of the ministry " (Eph. iv. 11, 12). From this distribution it would seem that a person might exercise one of these offices and none of the rest. He might be a prophet or evangelist, and not an apostle or pastor. But with us a clergyman is expected to be more or less of all, except an apostle. Let our church set about this distribution, this division of labor, and if the Holy Ghost be indeed in the midst of her dispensing His manifold gifts, and if she desires, above all things, rightly to use the dispensation of the gospel committed to her, she will find among her members prophets, evangelists, preachers, exhorters, and teachers, in men qualified to be such, and yet not calculated for, nor desiring admission to, the ranks of her regular ministry. Nor, if the Holy Ghost be in the midst of her, will she fail to discern prophets of the Holy Ghost in communions round about her, holding a faith identical with her own.—Discerning them will she hold no fellowship with them? Will she refuse to let her people hear them? Will she utterly ignore them? Rather will she not hail them as co-workers in spreading the gospel? Will she not show that she discriminates between them and others preaching in the name of Christ but not preaching His truth? To treat all prophets beyond her pale, true and false, alike; to regard the former with no more favor than the latter, may be very prudent, but hardly the dictate of zeal for the truth, or of confidence in its power for good, notwithstanding some admixture of error. It is well to protect the Gospel by our canonical inclosures, but not well to prevent it, on its free course around, from ever coming within.

No church could more consistently pursue the liberal course here pleaded for, than one which is so truly liberal in her spirit, and tolerates every variety of theological sentiment not at variance with the faith. One, too, which from her safeguards for the truth has so little to fear from contact with her neighbors. With her scriptural liturgy, at once her wall of defence, and touchstone for her people to "try the spirits," what damage could they take from a distasteful or erroneous expression by a more zealous than accurate preacher? Should her Arminian members occasionally hear a Calvinistic statement, or *vice versâ*, what more would it be than they now hear from her own preachers divided on those theologies? As an ancient branch of the Catholic Church, as Evangelical as Catholic, and venerated as such by her Protestant sisters, may she use the advantages of her acknowledged position among them, for a leading part in a joint advancement of the glory of her Lord and theirs.

I conclude with answering a practical objection which it is easy to anticipate: "Supposing the theory true, still the acting upon it would be a serious evil which would outweigh any possible good. Instead of listening for edification to their own pastors, people would be on the look-out for new preachers. 'What denomination are we to have to-day?' would be the question on going to church. It might suit the lovers of religious dissipation, but not grave and earnest worshippers." All this I grant, and worse, too, might follow, were it the custom for preachers, other than our own, to officiate at our regular services. But it is not that which is proposed, nor would that be desirable. Nothing should interrupt each communion proceeding with its stated rites and usages in its own way. The object is not to do away their differences which consist with their substantial oneness. Their several priesthoods, I mean their ministries celebrating the Christian rites after their own modes, exhibit their diversity —their owning a common preacherhood would manifest their unity, and their manifestation of this should be on special occasions for the purpose, and not, or rarely, on the ordinary occasions of public worship. The preacher would then address himself to a congregation who had come to hear the testimony from his mouth. If he delivered it in a right spirit they would have no right to be offended at any peculiarity he might fall into of theological dialect. It enlarges our capacity for the truth to hear its notes in the varied tones which it takes in different minds. Congregations of the Testimony, so to call them, might meet at convenient times, in the different houses of worship of the several consenting communions. And why not in our own? Why might not our churches be opened, at other times than those of their regular services, simply for the preaching of the Gospel, not, indeed, wholly without any acts of devotion, especially such as the singing of hymns, but mainly for the former as the great object in view? It would be on such occasions, when the churches should be free and open to all, mission churches for the time being, that discourses might be delivered, *ad populum*, by earnest and acceptable preachers of other churches, as well as by those of our own, at the invitation of the Rectors of the respective churches. Surely no harm could come of it, while the great good would be done of showing that underlying our church affection there is a deep affection for the truth by whomsoever proclaimed, and that with all our scrupulous observance of church order, we dare not disown the higher order of Him, who calls whom He wills to be prophets of His word. There would thus be an advance, I have proposed nothing more than an advance, towards union.* If even for that we are not ready, may the Lord, if it be for His glory, hasten it in His time.

W. A. M.

---

* The measure proposed in the "Memorial" for a free extension of Episcopal orders, looks to a catholic organization of the Evangelical churches, and is advocated in my Exposition of that document on the ground of consistency in our church. What is here pleaded for is independent of that, and might, on our part, be preparatory to it.

www.ingramcontent.com/pod-product-compliance
Lightning Source LLC
Chambersburg PA
CBHW021435090426
42739CB00009B/1491